YEAR R–1

Clas

Synthetic Phonics Photocopiable Readers

Helen Hadley

Nelson Thornes
a Wolters Kluwer business

Published in 2006 by:
Nelson Thornes Ltd
Delta Place
27 Bath Road
CHELTENHAM
GL53 7TH
United Kingdom

06 07 08 09 10 / 10 9 8 7 6 5 4 3 2 1

A catalogue record for this book is available from the British Library

ISBN 0-7487-8414-4

Cover photograph by Oliver Poole
Illustrations by Woody Fox and Jess Stockham
Page make-up by GreenGate Publishing Services

Printed in Great Britain by Ashford Colour Press

Classworks: Synthetic Phonics Photocopiable Readers

This book provides a large bank of photocopiable phonic readers. It is directly linked to *Classworks: The Synthetic Phonics Book* but can be used alongside any synthetic phonics scheme to provide low-cost, extra reading practice. Being copiable, the stories make ideal take-home resources.

It follows the build up of sounds in the *Classworks The Synthetic Phonics Book*, which, week by week, teaches children letters, consonant digraphs, vowel digraphs or letter clusters. Children also learn some common sight words. As this progression is similar to that found in most other synthetic phonic schemes, you will find the stories invaluable in your classroom with the new emphasis on structured phonic work.

In line with the 'first and fast' principles of synthetic phonics, *Classworks* covers all the main phonic rules in fifteen weeks. Starting from Week 2 this book has stories for each week: two for Week 2 and four or five from Week 3 onwards. Each story gives children practice in reading words in context, built from the letters they have learnt that week, as well as letters learnt in previous weeks, to aid fluent reading.

As in *Classworks: The Synthetic Phonics Book*, simple punctuation is used: commas, full stops, speech marks and exclamation marks, but not capital letters except for the word 'I'. To expect children to recognise both lower case and capitals for each letter (and when to use them) at the same time as learning the complexities of pronouncing letters and consonant clusters is just too much at this stage. We want children to be able to make immediate sound–symbol relationships, in order to work confidently and to use the knowledge they have gained so far. *Classworks: Synthetic Phonics Photocopiable Readers* provides children with the means to reinforce that learning.

Working with the stories

Discuss the title and the picture with the children. What do they think the story will be about? Go through the words in the boxes and talk about their meanings. These words focus on the letters, letter clusters and sight words learnt by the end of that week. They will remind children of the letters before they meet the words in the story. The words will also help them to read the story more fluently. Ask the children to read the story to you. Talk about the story and then ask them to read it again. Let the children take the stories home to read to their families so parents can see the progress being made and support what their child is doing in school. On the next page you will find a sample photocopiable letter that could be sent home to parents.

Dear Parent,

Your child will now start bringing home story pages to share with you. The words in these stories are built from the letters your child has learnt to date. The content is a bit limited at first but, as your child learns more letters and words, the stories become longer and more interesting.

Reading the stories

- First read the title of the story together.
- Talk about what is happening in the picture.
- Ask your child what they think the story will be about.
- Go through the words in the boxes and ask what they think the words mean. These words focus on the letters or letter clusters your child has learnt at school by the end of that week. They will remind your child of the letters before they meet the words in the story. This will help them to read the story more fluently.
- Ask your child to read the story to you.
- Talk about the story, then ask them to read it again.
- Give lots of praise to your child. Even if they make a mistake, there is always something you can praise.
- Encourage your child to colour in the pictures.
- Get a book to stick the stories in, or place them in a file, so they build up their own story book.
- Keep the book by your child's bed and encourage them to read the stories to themselves or to another family member.

I hope you will enjoy sharing these stories with your child. Through doing so you will become aware of the progress they are making and you will be helping them along the path to becoming a reader.

Yours faithfully

a rat and an ant

sal	rat	slid	sid	tin	din

sal is a rat.

sid is an ant.

sal and sid slid in a tin.

a rat and an ant in a tin.

sal and sid ran in a tin.

it is a din in a tin.

1. Say the words in the boxes.   2. Read the story.

Classworks: Synthetic Phonics Photocopiable Readers © Helen Hadley, Nelson Thornes Ltd, 2006

dan and a lid

rats	sit	lid	dan	lad	stands

ants sit in a lid.

rats sit in a lid.

dan is a lad.

dan stands at the lid.

"a! a! a! a! a!"

ants and rats ran.

dan sits in a lid.

1. Say the words in the boxes.   2. Read the story.

Classworks: Synthetic Phonics Photocopiable Readers © Helen Hadley, Nelson Thornes Ltd, 2006

2

dad's pet

| mel | nest | fed | felt | pest | flaps |

dad fed mel.

mel is dad's pet.

mel is in a nest.

mel felt an ant in its nest.

an ant is a pest.

mel flaps at an ant in its nest.

1. Say the words in the boxes.   2. Read the story.

ned's tent

sits	I	tent	damp	fat	stamp

ned sits in a tent.

I sit in ned's tent.

it is damp in ned's tent.

a fat ant is in ned's tent.

I stamp an ant in ned's tent.

1. Say the words in the boxes.   2. Read the story.

Classworks: Synthetic Phonics Photocopiable Readers © Helen Hadley, Nelson Thornes Ltd, 2006

sam, pip and the rats

I	sam	pip	den	rats	ten

I met sam and pip.

sam and pip and I sat in a den.

sam felt rats in a den.

"a! a! a! a! a!"

sam and pip and I ran.

ten rats sat in a den.

1. Say the words in the boxes.   2. Read the story.

Classworks: Synthetic Phonics Photocopiable Readers © Helen Hadley, Nelson Thornes Ltd, 2006

sad fred

| I | fred | mad | lad | felt | pat |

I met fred.

fred is a pal.

fred is a mad lad.

I sat in fred's den.

fred felt sad.

I pat fred.

1. Say the words in the boxes.   2. Read the story.

Classworks: Synthetic Phonics Photocopiable Readers © Helen Hadley, Nelson Thornes Ltd, 2006

lots of pets

| my | cat | dog | hen | rat | self |

I fed my pets.

I fed my cat and

my pet dog.

I fed my hen and

my pet rat.

I fed my self.

1. Say the words in the boxes.   2. Read the story.

Classworks: Synthetic Phonics Photocopiable Readers © Helen Hadley, Nelson Thornes Ltd, 2006

I sit

hen	pen	on	cat	hat	mat

a rat sits in a den.

a hen sits in a pen.

an ant sits on a log.

a cat sits in a hat.

I sit on a mat.

1. Say the words in the boxes.   2. Read the story.

Classworks: Synthetic Phonics Photocopiable Readers © Helen Hadley, Nelson Thornes Ltd, 2006

tom and greg

tom	dog	greg	soft	can	get

tom has a dog.

his dog is greg.

greg is his pet dog.

greg has a soft mat.

greg sits on his mat.

tom can get his dog a red dog tag.

1. Say the words in the boxes.   2. Read the story.

Classworks: Synthetic Phonics Photocopiable Readers © Helen Hadley, Nelson Thornes Ltd, 2006

my pets

| my | hal | log | peg | can | not |

my dog hal sits on a log.

my cat peg sits on a log.

an ant can sit on a log.

I can pat my dog hal.

I can pat my cat peg.

I can not pat an ant.

1. Say the words in the boxes.   2. Read the story.

Classworks: Synthetic Phonics Photocopiable Readers © Helen Hadley, Nelson Thornes Ltd, 2006

lost in the fog

bob	bad	the	hut	cut	twig

tim and I got lost in the fog.

the mist and fog is bad.

my dog bob got to us in the fog.

bob led us to my hut but

I cut my hand on a twig and

tim hit his hip on a log.

1. Say the words in the boxes.   2. Read the story.

Classworks: Synthetic Phonics Photocopiable Readers © Helen Hadley, Nelson Thornes Ltd, 2006

my dog vic

| best | vic | pug | beg | went | got |

my best pet is my dog vic.

vic is a pug.

my pug can run.

it can beg.

my pug vic went up on a log.

vic got a rat up on the log.

1. Say the words in the boxes.   2. Read the story.

Classworks: Synthetic Phonics Photocopiable Readers © Helen Hadley, Nelson Thornes Ltd, 2006

on the raft

| bud | the | raft | soft | val | wet |

my dad bud is on a raft.

dad sits on a soft pad.

my mum val is on the raft.

mum sits on a soft pad.

I am on the raft.

it is wet on the raft but

mum has a mop.

1. Say the words in the boxes.   2. Read the story.

Classworks: Synthetic Phonics Photocopiable Readers © Helen Hadley, Nelson Thornes Ltd, 2006

sand in dad's van

van	bev	fun	went	the	swept

dad has a van.

bev and I had a fun trip in dad's van.

dad and bev and I went on the sand.

bev and I went in to dad's van.

sand got in dad's van.

my dad swept up the sand in his van.

---

1. Say the words in the boxes.   2. Read the story.

Classworks: Synthetic Phonics Photocopiable Readers © Helen Hadley, Nelson Thornes Ltd, 2006

kip and the bun

| kip | rug | jam | to | yum | bad |

kip sat on the soft rug.

kip had a bun on the rug.

the bun had jam in it.

kip bit in to the bun, yum! yum! but

jam went on the rug.

yes, kip is a bad lad.

1. Say the words in the boxes.   2. Read the story.

Classworks: Synthetic Phonics Photocopiable Readers © Helen Hadley, Nelson Thornes Ltd, 2006

jim and viv and the milk

jug	milk	jim	yak	viv	zebra

mum went to get a jug of hot milk.

the milk kept hot in the jug.

jim had hot milk in his mug.

the mug had a yak on it.

viv had hot milk in a cup.

the cup had a zebra on it.

jim spilt the milk in his mug.

---

1. Say the words in the boxes.   2. Read the story.

Classworks: Synthetic Phonics Photocopiable Readers © Helen Hadley, Nelson Thornes Ltd, 2006

skip at the vet's

skip	to	jab	zap	yaps	yelps

my dog skip is not at his best.

skip went to the vet.

skip had a jab from the vet.

zap, the jab went in to his skin.

skip yaps and yelps.

I hug my dog skip.

1. Say the words in the boxes.   2. Read the story.

Classworks: Synthetic Phonics Photocopiable Readers © Helen Hadley, Nelson Thornes Ltd, 2006

my zig-zag

liz	jumps	jon	jog	ha	zig-zag

liz is my mum.

liz skips and jumps.

jon is my dad.

jon went on a jog.

I ran in a big zig-zag.

mum and dad went, "ha! ha! ha!"

it is fun to run in a zig-zag.

1. Say the words in the boxes.   2. Read the story.

Classworks: Synthetic Phonics Photocopiable Readers © Helen Hadley, Nelson Thornes Ltd, 2006

dad's shed

| chat | chin | of | shelf | latch | maths |

dad is a bit fed up.

dad sits with his chin in his hands.

"dad, let's sit in the shed."

dad lifts the latch of his shed to get in.

the shed has a bench in it and a shelf.

dad and I sit at the bench and chat.

dad helps me with my maths.

1. Say the words in the boxes.   2. Read the story.

patch has an itch

patch	stretch	itch	scratch	brush	of

patch is my dog.

patch runs and jumps up on the bench.

patch has a big stretch.

patch has an itch.

patch has to scratch it.

I brush patch to get rid of the itch.

patch has lots of ants on him.

the brush gets rid of them.

1. Say the words in the boxes.   2. Read the story.

my big fish

catch	fish	with	my	lunch	chips

dad and I went to the pond.

dad and I went to catch fish.

I had my rod.

dad got lots of fish.

I just got a fish but my fish is a big fish.

mum and dad and I had my big fish at lunch.

I had chips with my big fish.

1. Say the words in the boxes.   2. Read the story.

Classworks: Synthetic Phonics Photocopiable Readers © Helen Hadley, Nelson Thornes Ltd, 2006

the rich jam buns

josh	shop	fetch	of	such	rich

mum sent josh to the shop to

fetch the buns.

the buns with jam in them.

josh ran to mum with the buns.

mum had a cup of milk with a bun.

josh had a mug of milk with his bun.

yum, yum, such rich jam buns.

1. Say the words in the boxes.   2. Read the story.

lunch on the rocks

chad	tess	rocks	lunch	was	off

chad and tess went on the sand to the rocks.

chad and tess sat on a rock.

the lunch is on the bench.

a bunch of ants smell the lunch.

tess picks up her lunch.

a bunch of ants was on her lunch and on her hand.

tess yells, "yuck! yuck!" and runs off.

1. Say the words in the boxes.   2. Read the story.

Classworks: Synthetic Phonics Photocopiable Readers © Helen Hadley, Nelson Thornes Ltd, 2006

lunch at the mill

| mill | back | jeff | jock | sniffs | was |

I went up to the mill.

the mill is at the top of a hill.

I had lunch in my back pack.

my pal jeff ran up the hill to the mill.

his dog jock ran up with him.

jeff and I sat on the moss to munch lunch.

I rub jock's back.

jock sniffs and licks my hand.

it was fun.

1. Say the words in the boxes.   2. Read the story.

Classworks: Synthetic Phonics Photocopiable Readers © Helen Hadley, Nelson Thornes Ltd, 2006

the doll and the duck

doll	dress	muff	fell	duck	was

bess had a doll with a red dress and a muff.

bess got the doll at a shop.

bess went to the pond with the doll.

the doll fell in the pond with a plop.

a duck swam to the doll.

it swam back to bess with the doll.

the doll was wet but

bess was glad to get her doll back.

1. Say the words in the boxes.   2. Read the story.

Classworks: Synthetic Phonics Photocopiable Readers © Helen Hadley, Nelson Thornes Ltd, 2006

bad zack

| zack | bell | spills | jen's | yells | scruff |

zack the cat has a bell.

the bell hits a cup of milk.

the milk spills on to jen's dress and

as zack laps up the milk his bell snags the dress.

jen yells at zack.

jen grabs the scruff of zack's neck and

plops him on the rug.

jen is cross with zack.

zack is mad at jen.

---

1. Say the words in the boxes.   2. Read the story.

Classworks: Synthetic Phonics Photocopiable Readers © Helen Hadley, Nelson Thornes Ltd, 2006

dad and his duck

duck	for	next	junk	sprang	quack

dad had a duck for a pet.

dad and jack went to the pond with the duck.

next thing, dad's duck fell in the pond.

the pond had lots of junk in it.

the duck cut its leg and swam back to the bank.

dad bent down to catch the duck but

it sprang at him with a "quack, quack," and then ran off.

dad and I set off to catch the duck.

1. Say the words in the boxes.   2. Read the story.

Classworks: Synthetic Phonics Photocopiable Readers © Helen Hadley, Nelson Thornes Ltd, 2006

the swing

frank	trunk	swing	hung	fix	quick

frank and tess went up the trunk and

then on to a branch.

frank had to fix the swing that hung from the branch.

then frank went on the swing.

tess had a quick swing as well.

frank and tess went back to tell mum that

it was fun on the swing.

1. Say the words in the boxes.   2. Read the story.

Classworks: Synthetic Phonics Photocopiable Readers © Helen Hadley, Nelson Thornes Ltd, 2006

the bad dog

| tex | sprang | fangs | for | quick | thanks |

tex and his dad went up to the cliff.

next, a bad dog sprang at tex.

his fangs bit tex's leg.

tex's leg bled.

dad ran at the dog but

the dog ran off.

dad was quick to mop up tex's leg with a cloth.

tex thanks dad for his help.

1. Say the words in the boxes.   2. Read the story.

Classworks: Synthetic Phonics Photocopiable Readers © Helen Hadley, Nelson Thornes Ltd, 2006

jeff's trip

jeff	for	drink	dock	swing	next

jeff went to the shop for a snack and a drink then

jeff went on a ship for a trip.

the ship left the dock.

jeff sat on the deck to munch his snack and

drink his drink.

the ship began to swing in the wind.

next, jeff slid on the deck.

jeff grabs at a bench to stop.

jeff is glad to get back to the dock.

1. Say the words in the boxes.   2. Read the story.

Classworks: Synthetic Phonics Photocopiable Readers © Helen Hadley, Nelson Thornes Ltd, 2006

the pink bike

home	late	bike	rides	he	cute

dad came home late.

he came home with a bike.

the bike was pink.

the pink bike was for june.

dad held the bike as june rode on it.

he gave june lots of rides on the bike.

june rode up the hill on the bike with dad.

it was a cute bike.

it was fun on the cute pink bike.

---

1. Say the words in the boxes.   2. Read the story.

the bike ride

luke	kate	cave	bikes	rode	he

luke went with kate to the lake.

at the side of the lake is a cave.

luke likes to hide in the cave.

he and kate rode to the cave on bikes.

kate fell off the bike.

luke got off his bike to help kate.

kate had a bang on the nose.

kate's nose bled a bit.

luke and kate rode back home.

1. Say the words in the boxes.   2. Read the story.

Classworks: Synthetic Phonics Photocopiable Readers © Helen Hadley, Nelson Thornes Ltd, 2006

mike and the mess

| mike | take | plate | spoke | use | he |

mum and mike went to the shop to get fish and chips and take them back home.

mike picks up a plate of chips.

mike drops the plate and spills the chips.

the chips make a mess.

mum was cross and spoke to mike.

mum made mike use a dust pan and brush to

pick up the chips.

he had to wipe up the rest of the mess with a wet cloth.

1. Say the words in the boxes.   2. Read the story.

Classworks: Synthetic Phonics Photocopiable Readers © Helen Hadley, Nelson Thornes Ltd, 2006

duke and rose

duke	rose	dunes	mule	time	pile

duke and rose went to the sand dunes.

duke ran to the sand dunes.

most of the time rose ran with him but

this time rose rode on a mule.

duke and rose made a big pile with the sand.

rose got a wet dress.

duke takes rose back home on the mule.

1. Say the words in the boxes.   2. Read the story.

Classworks: Synthetic Phonics Photocopiable Readers © Helen Hadley, Nelson Thornes Ltd, 2006

jane, saba and the doll

| robe | jane | saba | dive | mine | waves |

jane sat on the grass with a doll.

the doll had on a long robe.

saba crept up to jane and

made a dive for the doll.

saba ran off with the doll.

"give it back," yells jane, "it's mine."

"no it is not," saba yells back, "it's mine."

mum waves at them and tells them to stop.

mum takes the doll from saba.

"I will take it back home," mum tells them.

1. Say the words in the boxes.   2. Read the story.

Classworks: Synthetic Phonics Photocopiable Readers © Helen Hadley, Nelson Thornes Ltd, 2006

scoop the dog

we	scoop	play	green	tail	soon

scoop is my dog.

scoop likes to play with his tail on the

green grass at the duck pond.

we stand on the bank and see lots of fish.

soon it is time for lunch.

I get food from my ruck sack.

I have a ham roll and a drink for lunch and

scoop has a bone.

1. Say the words in the boxes.   2. Read the story.

sam the snail

| snail | grass | weeds | spray | roots | tree |

sam the snail sat on the grass.

dad came on to the grass.

dad sees lots of weeds on the grass.

he gets a hose to spray the weeds

to get rid of them.

sam the snail did not like the spray.

he hid from the spray deep in the roots of a tree.

1. Say the words in the boxes.   2. Read the story.

jay and the black paint

| jay | paint | we | loops | tail | see |

jay is a bad lad.

he got black paint and a brush and

went to paint black loops on the cat's tail.

we see him paint the cat.

dad ran to jay to take the brush and

the paint from him.

the black paint on the brush went on dad's hands.

dad was cross with jay and sent him to bed.

1. Say the words in the boxes.   2. Read the story.

Classworks: Synthetic Phonics Photocopiable Readers © Helen Hadley, Nelson Thornes Ltd, 2006

the clay doll

ray	keeps	clay	pail	we	sweep

ray likes to make things with clay.

he keeps his clay in a pail.

ray made a doll with the clay.

we went to see the doll. it was sweet.

ray spilt clay on his feet.

he had to get a broom and sweep it up.

ray was not in a sweet mood.

mum was glad he swept up the clay.

1. Say the words in the boxes.   2. Read the story.

a bag of sweets

abid	sweets	teeth	says	pain	we

I went up on the green to meet my mate, abid.

he had a bag of sweets.

"want a sweet, des?" says abid.

"my mum says lots of sweets will rot my teeth."

"my mum says that too," agrees abid.

"shall we stop having sweets, abid?"

"that's a pain, des. I like sweets a lot."

"let's just suck three sweets a day," I say.

"we will see if we can stick to it," says abid.

will des and abid stick to just three sweets a day?

1. Say the words in the boxes.   2. Read the story.

Classworks: Synthetic Phonics Photocopiable Readers © Helen Hadley, Nelson Thornes Ltd, 2006

joan and rex

joan	hound	moist	she	brown	counts

joan takes out my hound rex to

roam on the hills.

the ground is moist so

she can not sit down.

joan counts five brown cows down on the bank and

six goats up on the hill.

the cows moo at joan as

she runs down the hill to take rex home.

---

1. Say the words in the boxes.   2. Read the story.

Classworks: Synthetic Phonics Photocopiable Readers © Helen Hadley, Nelson Thornes Ltd, 2006

roy and boyd

roy	toast	boyd	coast	boat	down

roy got up and had some toast then

he went to see his mate, boyd.

boyd and roy went down the coast in

a boat to catch fish.

the boys catch lots of fish but

then the rain came down.

roy and boyd need rain coats on.

the boys sail back home with the fish.

1. Say the words in the boxes.   2. Read the story.

Classworks: Synthetic Phonics Photocopiable Readers © Helen Hadley, Nelson Thornes Ltd, 2006

the pink crab

kay	down	we	found	joint	moan

kay and I run down to play on the sands.

"I have found a spade," I shout to kay.

we dig in the sand with the spade to

make a deep hole.

a big pink crab comes out of the sand.

I feel it pinch a bone on my hand, just on a joint.

I moan and shout, "ouch! ouch! ouch!"

1. Say the words in the boxes.   2. Read the story.

Classworks: Synthetic Phonics Photocopiable Readers © Helen Hadley, Nelson Thornes Ltd, 2006

the owl in the tree

moon	clouds	owl	hoot	she	joy

the moon came out from the clouds.

an owl went, "hoot, hoot."

joy went out to see the owl.

she found the owl up in a tree.

it was a brown owl.

joy went up to the tree but the owl went off.

she saw the owl take off and she was sad.

she went home and had a moan to her mum.

1. Say the words in the boxes.   2. Read the story.

the clowns

clowns	join	ground	boys	coach	crowd

the boys play in a match at the school ground.

jake, frank and mick dress up as clowns to

cheer on the boys.

mums and dads see the boys play.

the boys take a rest and

the coach gives them a drink.

the clowns have a drink and then

have fun and games with the crowd.

at the end of the match, the boys join

the clowns and play tag on the way home.

it was a fun day.

1. Say the words in the boxes.   2. Read the story.

Classworks: Synthetic Phonics Photocopiable Readers © Helen Hadley, Nelson Thornes Ltd, 2006

help! help!

dawn	brook	neal	dean	said	throw

I took dawn to play down at the brook.

we had fun but then dawn's foot slid on the wet bank and she fell in to the brook.

dawn screams and I said, "I will run to get help."

"neal! dean!" I shout. "dawn fell in the stream."

"help me get dawn out."

neal and dean take a rope with them and throw the rope to dawn.

she grabs the end of the rope.

neal and dean tug on the rope and get dawn out.

I throw my coat round dawn as we run home.

1. Say the words in the boxes.   2. Read the story.

Classworks: Synthetic Phonics Photocopiable Readers © Helen Hadley, Nelson Thornes Ltd, 2006

the boys go to camp

| took | show | way | beans | yawns | said |

yong and rick took jay to scout camp.

at camp the boys meet lots of scouts.

the scouts show jay the way to cook.

the boys eat a big meal of beans, chips and lean meat.

next, each boy eats a peach with cream.

then jay yawns, so yong said, "it is time to sleep."

the three boys, yong, rick and jay sleep in a tent.

1. Say the words in the boxes.   2. Read the story.

Classworks: Synthetic Phonics Photocopiable Readers © Helen Hadley, Nelson Thornes Ltd, 2006

bea's gift

bea	took	said	book	shows	draw

ray and jean went to see bea.

this is the day bea is six.

ray and jean took a gift for bea.

it was a book for bea to draw in.

bea smiles at them.

"is that for me?" she said.

bea likes her book and she shows it to her mum.

"thank you for my book," said bea.

"it will be good to have a book to draw in."

1. Say the words in the boxes.   2. Read the story.

dean, the rook and the book

dean	peas	cook	rook	bowl	smile

mum sends dean out to pick lots of peas.

she needs them to cook for lunch.

he picks a bowl of peas then hides at the back of the shed.

dean has a book with him. he sits on the ground to read it.

a rook creeps up to his bowl and pecks at the peas.

dean claps his hands to get rid of the rook.

then mum shouts, "dean, bring the peas to me."

dean hides his book and runs in to mum.

"thanks, dean," said mum.

dean has to smile. it was a good read.

1. Say the words in the boxes.   2. Read the story.

bea and the hawk

lawn	book	draw	claws	me	shows

bea went out on to the lawn.

she took a book and lots of felt pens.

bea says she will draw a hawk in the book.

she sits on the lawn and

draws a hawk with big claws on its feet.

she shows the book to mum.

dad came out. "let me have a look," he said.

"wow! that is a good hawk you have drawn."

1. Say the words in the boxes.   2. Read the story.

Classworks: Synthetic Phonics Photocopiable Readers © Helen Hadley, Nelson Thornes Ltd, 2006

a day at the beach

| burt | kirk | for | surf | they | burn |

dad took burt and kirk down to the beach in his car.

kirk went for a jog on the beach.

burt found lots of shells in the sand.

dad took the boys out to surf on the waves.

then they laid on the beach and fell asleep in the sun.

the sun was hot. dad woke up with a start.

"wake up, burt! wake up, kirk! your skin will burn red in

this hot sun," dad said as he shook the boys.

"it is not good to go to sleep in the sun!"

he put sun cream on the boys' skin to stop the sun burn.

---

1. Say the words in the boxes.   2. Read the story.

Classworks: Synthetic Phonics Photocopiable Readers © Helen Hadley, Nelson Thornes Ltd, 2006

the boys in the barn

| curt | mark | short | dark | yard | they |

curt and mark spot bart in the yard.

"let's go and hide from him in the barn," said curt.

they went in to the dark barn and hid in the cart.

bart looks for the boys in the yard.

a short sound came from the barn.

bart ran to the barn but it was dark in the barn.

he did not see the boys but the cart starts to shake.

bart looks in the cart and sees curt and mark.

"ha! ha! ha!" they shout. such a lot of fun they had that day.

1. Say the words in the boxes.   2. Read the story.

Classworks: Synthetic Phonics Photocopiable Readers © Helen Hadley, Nelson Thornes Ltd, 2006

the girl in the park

arim	park	fir	turf	hurl	they

min and arim went to the park to play with the hoop.

a girl stood next to a fir tree. she was sad.

min sent the hoop to the girl.

it hit a bump in the turf.

the girl ran to catch the hoop and

hurl it back to them.

they went up to the girl.

"will you come and play with us?" said arim.

"yes, I will," said the girl.

1. Say the words in the boxes.   2. Read the story.

a trip to the zoo

far	shark	sea	bird	stork	they

"mum, is it far to the zoo?" said jake.

"no," said mum, "not far."

"will we see a shark at the zoo?"

"no," said mum, "sharks swim in the sea."

"will we see a big bird like a stork, mum?"

"we may do," said mum, "but we will see birds."

jake said, "will we see a seal?"

"yes," said mum, "you will see lots of them in the lake."

they had a good time at the zoo.

1. Say the words in the boxes.   2. Read the story.

lorna's dog

bark	curl	dirt	jumps	cord	they

mum, lorna and the dog sit out side.

the dog starts to curl up in the soil and

make a mess of his fur.

mum jumps up from the seat and brushes the dirt from his fur.

"he's fine mum, it's just his fun," said lorna.

then the dog starts to bark and make a row.

"he makes far too much noise," said mum.

"take him for a run, lorna. he may be quite a good dog then."

"let's get off now," lorna said to the dog.

lorna has a cord as a lead and they set off for the park.

---

1. Say the words in the boxes.   2. Read the story.

Classworks: Synthetic Phonics Photocopiable Readers © Helen Hadley, Nelson Thornes Ltd, 2006

the flight to spain

flight	by	right	news	bright	her

mum, dad and beth left home by car to
catch the flight to spain.

they got to the plane right on time.

dad reads the news on the plane.

it took a long time to fly to spain.

they got to bed late that night.

they spent the next day on the beach.

it was hot in the bright sun shine.

dad saw beth was hot and said to her,

"let's get in the sea, it will be cool."

they had a good time in spain.

1. Say the words in the boxes.   2. Read the story.

Classworks: Synthetic Phonics Photocopiable Readers © Helen Hadley, Nelson Thornes Ltd, 2006

the witch, her cat and her hat

| witch | her | night | blew | fly | me |

the witch went up on the broom stick.

she had on a cloak and a hat as black as the night.

a black cat sat by her on the broom stick.

the wind blew hard and blew off the witch's hat.

the witch flew the broom stick down to the ground.

she said to the cat, "quick, quick, run and

fetch my hat for me!"

the wind blew hard and the cat had to chase the hat a

long way.

in the end he got it and gave it back to the witch.

"let's fly!" said the witch and up they flew into the sky.

1. Say the words in the boxes.   2. Read the story.

the lost bag

| fern | bert | threw | try | might | sharp |

bert and fern took her dog rex to the wood.

bert threw a stick for rex but it went in to the trees.

"that was not a good try," said fern but

rex came back with a bag in his mouth.

"fern, fern," said bert, "rex has found a hand bag."

"look in the bag, a name might be in it," said fern.

the name in the bag was rose sharp and

her home was at 5 short street.

fern and bert took the bag back to rose sharp.

rose gave a cry. "that's my bag!" she said.

she was glad to get her bag back.

1. Say the words in the boxes.   2. Read the story.

let's feed the birds

gail	dirk	they	fright	flew	her

mum said, "let's drive to the park and feed the birds."

gail had a short skirt on, a new top and a red scarf.

dirk had a light shirt on and dark shorts.

they saw lots of birds in the park.

they took nuts to feed the birds.

lots of birds flew down to the ground to eat the nuts.

mum, gail and dirk like to watch the birds feed.

a sharp sound gave the birds a fright and they flew off.

gail began to cry. she said to her mum,

"oh mum, the birds have flown up in to the sky."

1. Say the words in the boxes.   2. Read the story.

Classworks: Synthetic Phonics Photocopiable Readers © Helen Hadley, Nelson Thornes Ltd, 2006

down on the farm

farm	night	by	few	yard	we

dad drove us down to the farm.

it was a long way.

it was night by the time we got to the farm.

the next day we saw quite a few things.

a herd of cows went, "moo! moo!"

a hen in the yard went, "cluck! cluck!"

we like it down on the farm.

1. Say the words in the boxes.   2. Read the story.